# *The Little Book of Common Sense*

## ... or Pause for Thought with Wogan

### TERRY WOGAN

An Orion paperback

First published in Great Britain in 2014
by Orion
This paperback edition published in 2016
by Orion
an imprint of the Orion Publishing Group Ltd.
Carmelite House, 50 Victoria Embankment,
London EC4Y 0DZ

An Hachette UK company

1 3 5 7 9 10 8 6 4 2

A CIP catalogue record for this book is available
from the British Library.

ISBN 978-1-4091-4657-5

Printed and bound in Great Britain by
CPI Group (UK) Ltd, Croydon, CR0 4YY

www.orionbooks.co.uk

Sir Terry Wogan, KBE, was born in Limerick. After leaving college, he went into banking and five years later joined RTÉ as a newsreader/announcer. In 1969, Terry stood in for BBC Radio's Jimmy Young and later that year he was given his own daily shows on BBC Radio 1 and 2. In 1972, he took over the prestigious morning show slot. Terry's extensive television credits include his live chat show series *Wogan*, *Eurovision Song Contest*, *Come Dancing* and, of course, *Children in Need*, to name but a few. The Queen honoured him with a knighthood in 2005. Terry sadly passed away in January 2016, leaving behind his wife, Helen, and two sons and a daughter.

*Don't sweat the small stuff – only kindness matters.*

# *Introduction*

—⁓⁓⁓—

Please don't think that this slim volume has been thrown together in an idle moment, just because it lacks bulk. Admittedly, it's no *War and Peace*, but then, how many can claim to have made it to the end of that epic tale? I'm a believer in brevity, and this certainly fits the bill. I'll go so far as to say that an intelligent person like yourself will read it in no time at all. But to paraphrase a television programme title of my younger days:

*Never mind the width, feel the quality.*

This is not a book to put aside, saying, 'Well I've finished that, where's the latest Hilary Mantel?' This little work is designed to bring you back, again and again, to refresh your view and attitude to life, living and everything in between. You will find no easy answers to your dilemmas here, rather an alternative view of how to approach them.

Or to be honest, just my view – but you never know, you might even agree with me . . .

Terry Wogan

# *Life*

—⟨ϕϕ⟩—

One day at a time. But look where you're going –
particularly on a bike.

# *Time*

～∾∾∾～

We are told that it waits for no man; a winged arrow, hurtling us through the Universe. Like the White Rabbit, we must be here, there and everywhere, on time. Well, as they say in Ireland, 'When God made time, He made plenty of it'.

On a little road in Limerick, a stranger observed a farmer walking a pig to market. Given the nature of pigs, it was no easy task, the animal running all over the road. The stranger said to the farmer, 'Why don't you put the pig into the back of a van?', 'Why would I do that?' asked the farmer. 'Why, to save time, of course,' said the stranger. The farmer looked askance. 'Sure,' he said, 'and what does a pig know of time . . . ?'

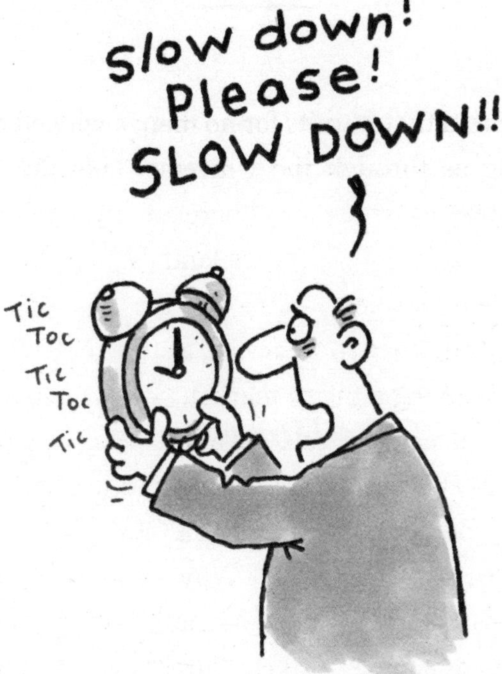
Slow down!
Please!
SLOW DOWN!!
Tic
Toc
Tic
Toc
Tic

## *God*

Never admit that you don't believe, particularly on Irish television. I've been having letters from nuns ever since . . .

## *Honesty*

Only works with strangers and people you hope never to meet again. With family and friends, keep your personal opinions to yourself. Unless you want to hear some hurtful home truths about yourself.

# *Lies*

—⦅◈◈⦆—

Keep them little, white and simple; otherwise you're bound to be caught out. I know you think you're inscrutable, but believe me, your face is an open book to the rest of us.

# *Truth*

—⟨ഗ⟩—

Leave plain speaking to Yorkshire men. 'Speaking as you find' is what's caused most of the trouble in the world. 'I'm only rude to people I like', is the proud boast of someone who doesn't understand why he hasn't a friend in the world.

# *Selfishness*

————— ❦ —————

Doesn't exist. Ask anybody and they'll tell you that if they have a fault, it's thinking too much of others.

## Regrets

———⁓⁓⁓———

Don't look back. You'll walk into a lamp post.

## Revenge

———⁓⁓⁓———

Not worth it. Unless you're Sicilian.

# *Relationships*

———∞∞∞———

Nobody knows anything. Just go for it and pray. Like life, it needs more luck than judgement.

## *Sex*

—⟨∞⟩—

Invented in the latter part of the last century by Helen Gurley Brown and *Cosmopolitan* magazine. Before that, everyone was happy with romance.

## *Love*

—⟨∞⟩—

Beauty, physical attraction, eyesight, knees, hair, all fade with time. Only kindness matters . . .

# *Romance*

———⟨◦/◦/◦⟩———

Blossomed during the Crusades, when troubadours sang of love to ladies whose lovers were far away and who had strapped them into chastity belts before they left. Also popular in the Ireland of my youth, where sex was only in it's infancy.

# *Chocolate*

———

Preferable to sex. You can have chocolate in front of your mother.

# *Heartbreak*

———

Don't risk it. Stay home with your mother. Or get a pet. At least animals will never let you down.

## *Women*

———◦◦◦———

Hopeless judges of men – see any family TV sitcom.
Can never be told the truth about their bums.

## *Men*

———◦◦◦———

No man can ever be told that he's bad in bed, behind
a wheel, or has no sense of humour . . .

# *Children*

—◦◦◦—

It's always the parents' fault.

# *Teenagers*

—⟨ഗ⟩—

I was one once, but didn't know it – they hadn't been invented. And I never saw a banana until I was 10. They don't know they're born . . .

# *In-laws*

—⁓—

As with outlaws and byelaws, watch your step.

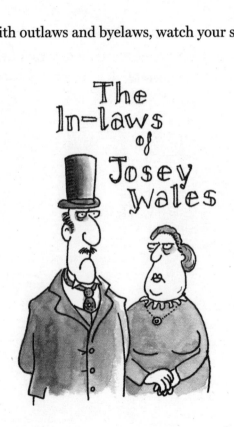

## Parties

—◦◦◦—

My youth was spent in the kitchen while others drank
the booze I'd brought. Or on a deserted beach, with
the last of the women and the burned barbecued
sausages long gone . . .

## Booze

—◦◦◦—

What are you having? We might as well be drunk as
the way we are.

# *Politicians*

Remember the nerdy ones in school?

# *Gambling*

———⌀⌀⌀———

The only known antidotes are the Paddy Power and
Victor Chandler bookie ads on satellite TV. I guarantee
they'll put you off for life . . .

# *Money*

———⌀⌀⌀———

Save or spend? Risk is for derivative and hedge fund
wonks. And it's not their money, anyway. Hold on to
your hard-earned ha'pennies, your children are going
to need them.

# *Online Dating*

—◊◊◊—

Only for the desperate. Get out more, talk to people and smile. It's worth a try.

# *Career*

—◊◊◊—

If you're a success, never forget how much of it you owe to luck. I remarked on this to a captain of industry, who was affronted at the very idea. He thought it was all due to him. It's a game of chance, and if the chips fall your way, pick them up and count them. Along with your blessings . . .

# *Success*

———⟨♨⟩———

Just like fame, a fickle jade. Short-lived and fleeting, unless you've got the vital element: luck. There's no such thing as an ever-rising curve, at some point, the law of diminishing returns sets in. Every boom is followed by a bust. Unfortunately, nobody told Gordon Brown, Lehmann's, the Chairman of the Bank of England and the property speculators of Ireland and Spain. They still don't believe it in Greece . . .

## *'I'm Good'*

The common reply these days to the solicitous inquiry, 'How are you?'. For Heaven's sake! You're not being asked about your moral behaviour, it's a civil question about your health. 'I'm fine', 'I'm never without pain' or 'fit as a butcher's dog', are the simple answers required.

# *Technology*

Never sent a tweet in my life.

# *Talk*

Only if you must. Keep it short and to the point. You don't want people to think you're a politician. Nobody wants a conversation in a lift, on the Tube, on a bus, on a plane, at the top of a back-swing, reading or writing, or when your mouth's full – button it. Pretend you're meeting the Queen; speak only when you're spoken to . . .

# *Manners*

———৵৶৶———

What used to be called 'good manners' is now regarded as mere affectation. Open a door for a young woman, and she's likely to call security . . .

# *Humour*

—◦◦◦—

See the entry on 'Talk'. Brevity is the soul of wit. You can't tell jokes like the late Les Dawson. He was funny. It's not a gift given to many. Just keep it short and snappy.

# *Listening*

—◦◦◦—

The most popular person at a party is the listener – particularly at an Irish party.

## Punchlines

⸺⟋⟍⸺

Preferable to a long-winded joke. My favourite:
'All right. But don't push me past me mother's . . . '

## Luck

⸺⟋⟍⸺

It's a lottery.

## Lottery

⸺⟋⟍⸺

It's luck.

Luck if you've ever been a lottery to begin with - Luck be a lottery toniiight

# *Talent*

—⟨ɷ⟩—

When complimented on a good shot, the great golfer Gary Player always said:

'The more I practice, the luckier I get'. Engagingly modest but ultimately untruc. Hard work and practice can take you to a certain level, but after that, only talent can take you any further.

# *Fame*

—⟨ɷ⟩—

Even if you do win *The X Factor*, nobody in China will ever have heard of you. And don't think you'll walk into the best table in a London restaurant. The receptionists are all foreigners, and they haven't heard of you either.

# *Eurovision Song Contest*

———∽∾∽———

Nothing more clearly defines the irreconcilable difference between ourselves and our fellows in the European community. They think that it's a feast of fine pop music. We think it's a joke . . .

# *Celebrity*

———— ❧ ————

Like 'Star', 'Genius' and 'Talent', a word that has lost all meaning.

# *Fashion*

———∽∾∽———

The last time I saw a pair of legs like that they were standing in a nest . . .

# *Acting*

———⟨∞⟩———

'Don't put your daughter on the stage, Mrs Worthington!'

Not unless she's ready for constant rejection, has a backbone of tungsten, and can live with starvation, frustration and envy. Even as we speak, I imagine Gwyneth Paltrow or Brad Pitt fretting over a part that should have been theirs. Never forget how many actors it takes to change a light bulb: One. And one to stand beneath the ladder, whining, 'That should be me up there . . .'

# *Media*

---

The last refuge for the show-off and the charlatan.
Stay away. There's only room for a few of us . . .

# *TV*

---

Cops, Hospitals, Cooking, Gardening, Reality, Atten-
borough, Miranda and Balding.

# *TV Golden Rule 1*

———⁄⁄⁄———

In all family sitcoms, fathers are idiots.

# *Golden Rule 2*

———⁄⁄⁄———

In all family sitcoms, mothers are smart, witty and the boss.

# *Talk show*

---

American TV expression. In the UK, it's a 'chat show'. More accurately, in Holland it's called a 'praat show'...

# Daytime TV

In contrast to the arid wastes of primetime, a source of hidden and remembered pleasures: *Poirot*, *The Good Life*, *Keeping Up Appearances*, *Murder She Wrote* (they must have made ten thousand episodes) and the present Lady Wogan's favourite, *Escape to the Country*, where a house-hunting couple is shown three different properties in beautiful locations and never, ever, buy one. It's the bucolic version of the big-money quiz, *The Chase*, where I've never seen a contestant win a brass farthing.

# *Radio*

The home of the introverted egomaniac. What sane person would think that they could keep millions of listeners entertained for hours on end, just by talking at them?

# Books (1)

—∽∾∾—

Hardly had my last tome hit the shelves before I received this:

'Over the weekend in my local bookshop, a young lad, summoning up his courage, eventually asked for a packet of condoms as he was too embarrassed to buy a copy of your book . . .'

# Books (2)

—∽∾∾—

At a book signing in Reading, I was surprised to be asked by a young man to sign a religious card. Seeing my puzzlement, the assistant explained, 'He thought you were Terry Waite . . .'

## Books (3)

———⁓⁓⁓———

At another signing, I'm surrounded by large photos of myself and book, my name writ large. I hear an old man say to an assistant: 'Who is it?'

## Books (4)

———⁓⁓⁓———

In Belfast, a smartly dressed man sporting a coat, corduroys, hat and umbrella, walks up to the desk where I'm signing. 'You're a lickspittle!' he shouts and turns to the door . . . 'A lickspittle!' he emphasises as he leaves.

# *Psychopath*

Glib, grandiose, cunning, shallow, parasitic, irresponsible, promiscuous. Commonly found in theatre, film and television.

# *Intelligence*

—◦◦◦—

Nobody's good at everything – you could be a late developer. I'll bet Albert Einstein never got a birdie in his life . . .

## *Footprints on the Sands of Time*

—————

Forget it. When did the names of Napoleon, Wellington, Alexander or Cicero last come up in the snug?

## *Art*

—————

'Anything that you can get away with.'

—Andy Warhol

# *Beige*

Otherwise known as 'fawn' or 'buff'. According to numpties, the colour of the non-descript and those well-stricken in years. Recently vindicated by scientific research as the true colour of the universe.

A stave from a long-lost poem:

*'I'm looking for someone in beige,*
*Someone with a pulse and a rather large wage,*
*Someone who'll warm my feet up at night,*
*Someone who'll tell me I'm looking all right,*
*Someone who's not at that desperate age,*
*I'm looking for someone in beige . . .'*

# Counter-intuitive

—◦◦◦—

Newly fashionable word, now freely in use at every committee and board meeting. May well mean 'not thinking before speaking' or more likely, just 'not thinking'. Which is much the same as . . .

# *Blue-sky Thinking*

⸺◦◦◦⸺

Involves consultants or advisers looking at the ceiling while waiting for the clouds that are befuddling the brain to clear, or the effects of a good lunch at the expense of the tax payer. Usually leads to a restful nap until the sky has darkened sufficiently to preclude further thought for the day.

## *Thinking Outside the Box*

—ᴓᴓ—

Vital if you are to avoid the off-side trap.

## *Thinking Inside the Box*

—ᴓᴓ—

Not much in evidence, unless you're looking for a penalty.

## Human Resources

Along with health and safety, council regulations on waste disposal and bus lanes, brings on the hopeless shrug. However did we manage to struggle on without a proper concern for ethnic diversity, inclusivity, team spirit and the rest of the H.R. brief? If ever asked what you would bring to the team, resist the urge to reply, 'A new striker and the half-time oranges'.

## Retirement

'Lift your feet! The carpet won't clean itself . . . '

# *Old Age*

—⚬⚬⚬—

Doesn't exist any more. 'Senior Citizen' and 'Silver Surfer' are the new euphemisms. Unless you're a female presenter on TV, in which case you're ready for the knacker's yard at 35.

# *Ailments*

It's remarkable how many people, despite the advances in medicine achieved over the years, still prefer to take their chances with health-food stores, homeopathy, herbal remedies, crystals and every passing guru and witch doctor, rather than the local GP. It's an ancient tradition not to trust the doctor. Here are some old cures that my more elderly listeners swear were practiced on them as children . . .

# Cold, Catarrh

———

Rub the chest with a brick.

# *Whooping Cough*

---

A piece of rope, soaked in tar, around the neck.

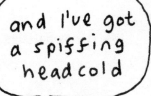

# *Stiff Neck*

———

Use a flatiron, over brown paper.

# *Earache*

An onion in hot ashes until soft, in the ear, with a white cloth tied around the head.

## Sore Knee

———∾∾∾———

A hot bread poultice. This I can personally vouch for
. . . never did me any harm . . . although I do limp a
little in cold weather.

# *Exercise*

———

In view of the indisputable fact that we all have a finite number of heartbeats, it seems foolhardy in the extreme to cause the old ticker to pound away at double and treble it's normal rate in gyms, on running tracks, on bicycles and marathons. Logically, too much physical exercise would seem the shortest route to an early grave.

An example from the natural world strengthens the case: I have personally fed a lettuce leaf to the longest-living creature on the planet, the Giant Tortoise of the Seychelles, at least 200 years old, and in all that time, he has hardly moved a muscle. Maybe a good argument for vegetarianism, but not for exercise . . .

## *Dieting*

———✦———

Don't be silly. There isn't a pick on you.

## *Sport*

———✦———

Becks has done OK, but the great cricketer, C.B. Fry, was offered the Kingdom of Albania – and without constantly showing off his underwear.

THE
*CB Fry*
UNDERGARMENT

# *Adventure*

———

Bungee jumping, skydiving, abseiling, snow boarding, ski jumping, bull fighting, crocodile wrestling, cage fighting, knitting, chess, origami and a million other dangerous pursuits that they tell me will make me feel more alive – are not for little me. I'm not sure how to check my adrenalin, but my pulse tells me I'm still alive. I'd prefer to remain that way. Throw another log on the fire . . .

# *Travel*

⸺◈⸺

'Better to travel than arrive.'

Not that you've any chance of arriving, if more than a half-inch of snow has fallen on Britain's airports . . . or leaves on the railway lines. But then, you've no chance of travelling, either.

## Public Transport

—◦◦◦—

I haven't been on a bus in thirty years, and if all those empty buses clogging London's streets mean anything, neither has anyone else.

## Road Rage

—◦◦◦—

How is any motorist expected to stay sane, in the face of road tax, congestion charges, speed cameras, bus lanes, traffic cones and potholed roads?

OFF-ROAD RAGE...

# *Motorways*

———

A cunning plan by the Highways Agency to keep drivers off the roads: bus lanes, out-of-date messages on the matrices, speed restrictions to deliberately slow the traffic-flow and the dreaded cones that still close miles of motorway lanes with no discernible activity on the other side. Such was the public fury, the Highways Agency set up a 'cones hotline' number, where drivers, driven to distraction, could ring to complain. Everyone who did was calmly told that their complaint was a mistake, and they were quite, quite wrong . . . it didn't help.

# *Americanisms*

———✦———

'I've a right to have a gun. Those damned Redcoats could attack at any moment.'

# *Holidays*

—⚬⚬⚬—

I've never been in a tent in my life, even in childhood I steadfastly refused to join the Boy Scouts. Sitting around a campfire, toying with a sausage that's burnt on the outside and raw inside never appealed. I've never been in a caravan, either. In a space no larger than a box-room, there's a loo, kitchen, washbasin, sitting room, diner and bedroom – a sure recipe for homicide. And why anybody would want to be less comfortable on holiday than they are at home remains a mystery.

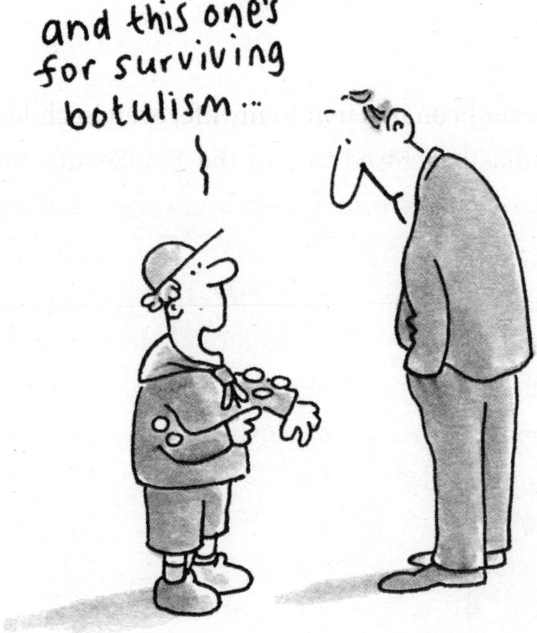
and this one's for surviving botulism...

# *Hi!*

'Hello' in Scandinavia.

# *Hi! Hi!*

'Goodbye', same place.

This easy familiarity with the languages of northern climes comes about because of the current obsession with Scandinavian television drama. *Borgen*, *The Killing* and *The Bridge* have not only impressed with their gloom and their knitwear, but their extraordinary guttural tongues. There we were, thinking Sweden, Denmark and Norway were as one and it turns out that they all speak a different language. Further, the Swedes think the Danes are chancers, the Danes think the Swedes are boring and both think the Norwegians should stick to the fjords. 'Hi!' and 'Hi! Hi!' are all they have in common.

# *Badgers*

—◦◦◦—

Regarded as lovable creatures of the wild, until it turned out that they eat hedgehogs.

## *Foxes*

Similarly regarded by the anthropomorphic city dweller, until it turned out that they don't just eat chickens, but people.

# *Fur*

——ᴐⱱⱱᴄ——

Apart from a badger cull, nothing more agitates the concerned citizen. A young lady wearing a fake fur, notices another, older woman in the room looking daggers at her. 'Don't worry,' she says placating, 'it's acrylic'. 'Well,' sniffs the other, 'we're all God's creatures ... '

# *Horses*

Noble animals that we've been eating for years without knowing it.

# *Organic Food*

Protect the temple that is your body from the contamination of pesticides and chemicals, and save the planet at the same time.

Except that recent research at Oxford University appears to show that organically produced milk, cereals and meat generate higher greenhouse gas emissions than the conventionally farmed. Back to the drawing board! Who's going to tell Prince Charles?

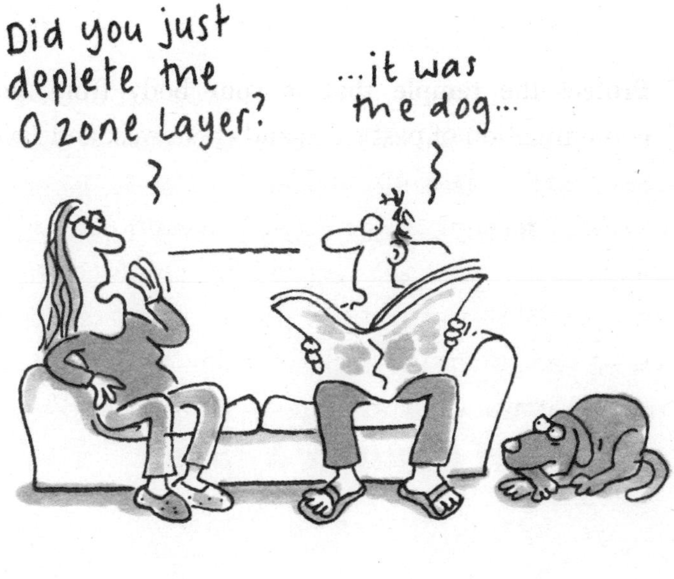
Did you just deplete the O zone Layer?
...it was the dog...

# Sardines, Pilchards and Bloaters

—⟨∽⟩—

Staples of my youth. When were you last offered a tasty sardine, pilchard sandwich or bloater paste? Don't tell me that they've gone the way of the non-sustainable cod? Get me Hugh Fearnley-Whittingstall!

# A Country Supper

—⟨∽⟩—

Last night's leftovers in a stew.

# A Good Lunch

—⟨∾⟩—

There was no such thing when I was a lad and not because my mother wasn't much of a cook. There was no such thing as 'lunch'. It was 'dinner'. It was at one o'clock and 'tea' was at six o'clock. There was no such thing as 'supper', either. There still isn't as far as I'm concerned – it's just an excuse for lazy cooks.

# *Supper on a Tray*

For those who'd rather watch the television than eat.

# *Baking*

———*෧౦෧*———

Stand-up comedy was known as 'the new Rock 'n' Roll', until the old Rock 'n' Rollers, scenting cash to keep them from the nursing home, started 'revival' touring and reclaimed the crown. Now it has been usurped once more, and this time by baking, and its heroine – the Queen of Cakes, Mary Berry – arise, Baroness Berry of Bakewell!

# *Posh*

Used to mean 'Port Out, Starboard Home', for those hardy souls sailing to the Colonies and for dear Mrs Bouquet, a house with a Mercedes and 'room for a pony'. Now it just means a painfully thin young woman with a huge handbag who never smiles . . .

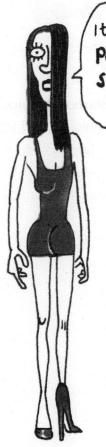

# Best of British

Epitomised by the former England cricket captain, Ted Dexter. Interviewed on a gantry outside the commentary box during a Test, while under an umbrella during an electrical storm.

Interviewer: 'What do you make of it so far, Ted?' A momentary pause, followed by Ted: 'You'll have to excuse me. I've just been struck by lightning'. Keep your James Bonds . . .

# *Irish Pubs*

———◦◦◦———

You can't turn a corner in any town from Ulan Bator to Minsk without running into an 'Irish Pub', usually called 'Scruffy Murphys' or 'Katie O'Rourkes'. All share one characteristic with the Blarney Stone: no self-respecting Irishman will ever be found within a mile of one.

# *Blarney*

---

If you wish to infuriate your friendly neighbour-
hood Irishman, call him 'Paddy' and describe his
conversation as 'Blarney'. Only numpties and tourists
hang by their ankles to kiss the Blarney Stone, a lump
of rock in an Irish castle, liberally covered in saliva
and lipstick.

# *Weather*

A reliable conversational standby, when the going gets tough over lunch at the in-laws. Otherwise a fruitful source of scorn that 'climate change' advocates are able to predict confidently that in 10 years time, we'll all be growing cacti instead of flowers – that's if we're not up to our shoulder-pads in water; while the Met Office seems incapable of telling us what the weather will be like the day after tomorrow.

# *Climate Change*

—◦◦◦—

Used to be known as 'global warming' until it became apparent that the planet was not turning into a shrivelled husk, as predicted by the doom-mongers. As the ice melts in the Arctic, so it grows colder in the Antarctic. Maybe it's not all our fault . . . whatever happened to Al Gore?

# *Globalisation*

—⟨⟨⟨⟨⟩⟩⟩⟩—

I have a friend who maintains that the world would be a better place if everybody stayed on their own side of the street.

# *Wind Turbines*

———⁓∾∾∾⁓———

I'm sure there's a joke in there somewhere about how many wind turbines it takes to turn on a light bulb . . .

insert your
caption here →

# *Aliens*

—⦿⦿⦿—

It all started with Orson Wells' *War Of The Worlds* radio spoof, which frightened America half to death in the 1930s. Since then we've gone from lights in the sky, to flying saucers, to . . .

# *Crop Circles*

———

Never mind that the most distinguished scientist in space research, Carl Sagan, says that our chances of being discovered by an alien civilisation is about the same as someone picking a single grain of sand from a beach, some still believe that the patterns drawn in the wheat fields of Wiltshire are the work of extraterrestrials. So, even if they come from the nearest galaxy, it's taken them light years, and a couple of generations to get here. They then draw pretty patterns in an obscure cornfield and fly back, their grandchildren arriving many light years later, to Andromeda Nebula and home. Imagine the welcome: 'You've been gone a hundred years and you've done WHAT?'

## *And finally . . .*

What, finished already? But then, as Ian McEwan and Shakespeare put so well, 'brevity is the soul of wit'. It's my excuse, anyway.

As I may have said elsewhere in this slim volume, only Tolstoy and Les Dawson could hold the attention for long periods. And, before you start picking holes in the finely-wrought fabric of these deeply-felt insights into the warp and woof of the daily grind, I know as well as you that one man's common sense is another's common place . . .